One Breast To Love And Living Life Victoriously

One Breast To Love And Living Life Victoriously

Tina Maria Scott

ISBN: 1532868448
ISBN 13: 9781532868443
Library of Congress Control Number: 2016906952
CreateSpace Independent Publishing Platform
North Charleston, South Carolina

Disclaimer

SOME OF THE NAMES WERE changed by the author to protect each individual's privacy.

Table of Contents

CHAPTER 1

The Diagnosis That Numbed Me

DURING A WARM MORNING SHOWER as I washed under my left armpit, I felt a lump the size of a pearl. I immediately put the soap down and gave my left armpit my full attention. I began to take deep breaths as I continued to hold the lump between my right index and middle fingers. I thought, "Oh, this is probably another cyst." I completed my warm shower and forgot about the lump until it was time to cleanse my body again. Each day during my shower or bath, I would examine under my armpit to see if the lump was going down.

After about a month of examining under my left armpit, the lump had not dissolved, so, I decided that I have enough of God's power within me to pray it away. As I remembered reading in the Bible, that God has given me power, I began praying daily, expecting the pearl-size lump to disappear.

Well, month two arrived, and there was no evidence of the lump vanishing. After two months of praying, I thought, "Well, I better go to the doctor to see what is really going on."

When I saw the doctor, he asked how long, had I felt the growth, and I said about two months. After examining my armpit, the doctor told me that I should see a surgeon to determine exactly what the growth was. I said, "Ooh, no, I do not want to see a surgeon right now. I'm trusting that it is just a cyst, so I am going to keep praying, trusting that it will go away."

After my office visit within about two weeks, I noticed that my left armpit was turning black and expelling a strong, rotten fragrance. It was an offensive smell—one that even soap and deodorant could not overpower.

I called my doctor for an urgent appointment and was blessed to be seen right away. As the doctor was examining my left armpit, I was told that the blackness under my armpit was maybe because I was overweight.

I know disbelief was written all over my face, as I was hearing the doctor say the blackness was maybe because I was overweight. I said to myself in a low voice, "That is not true." The doctor's explanation of why my armpit was black definitely did not make sense to me. I thought, "I am overweight but not that overweight, and I do not have folds of skin under my armpit that could possibly cause discoloration." My sensitivity thought, "What a mean thing to say!"

The doctor suggested once again that I see a surgeon to determine exactly what the growth was, and I agreed. I left my appointment feeling jolted by the doctor's explanation of why my armpit was black.

Unfortunately, I took the comment to heart because I already knew that I was approximately twenty-five pounds heavier than I desired. On my way home, I thought about how I judged the doctor's comment and then did some self-reflecting. I knew it was much deeper than the doctor's statement, especially since in the past, he had always been kind and gone the extra mile to order different tests to make sure that my complaints were addressed accurately and showed nothing but concern for me.

I had to admit to myself that I was jolted because I was not comfortable with the excess body weight that I had been saying I wanted to release for a long time, and perhaps it was true that one could have black discoloration under the armpit due to being overweight.

One thing I knew for sure was that the doctor did not intentionally try to jolt me. Deep down I knew that no one could make me feel jolted except me, and maybe I needed to feel jolted so that I could do something about the excess weight.

The following morning when I arrived at work I called the surgery department, and a polite and energetic young woman greeted me. I told the young woman that I wanted a Friday appointment, and she replied, "The next Friday appointment is on the thirteenth! Do you want to come on Friday the thirteenth?"

I laughed and said, "I sure do, because I am not superstitious," and then we both laughed!

The young woman proceeded to make my appointment by asking me whom I would like to see. I told her that I was new to the area and was not familiar with any of the surgeons. I asked her if she would schedule me an appointment with the surgeon she would select for herself. She said okay in a cheerful voice.

She stated that Dr. Artistry was the best surgeon that they have and that I would be pleased with him. The young woman also told me that he was well sought after! Feeling her smile through the telephone, I felt like I would be in good hands, so I agreed to see Dr. Artistry. She scheduled the appointment for Friday, August 13, 2010, and wished me good luck with my medical diagnosis.

I had approximately one-and-a-half weeks before my appointment with Dr. Artistry. During the waiting period, I examined my left armpit daily to feel if the pearl-size lump was shrinking. I thought, "What is really going on? After all the praying I've been doing, this lump should be gone by now!" The lump had not shrunk any; actually it felt larger than it did a week and a half ago!

I began to feel a little anxious about my upcoming appointment with the doctor. Well, Friday, August 13, 2010, finally arrived! I walked into the examination room and went through the normal routine of being asked why I was there today. I shared with the medical assistant that I had a lump under my left armpit and under my armpit was very dark with a horrible odor. The medical assistant typed into the computer what I had shared with her and then told me the doctor would be in soon. She handed me a top gown and told me to put it on, and then left the room.

My mother was with me during this examination. As soon as the medical assistant left the room, my mother asked how I was feeling. I admitted that I was feeling really nervous! My mother could sense that I was feeling disturbed by the growth, rotten fragrance, and darkness under my armpit, so she tried to console me by saying, "Don't worry; you are fine!" She did not say everything will *be* fine, she said, *you are fine.* Dr. Artistry came into the examination room in less than ten minutes. He said hello and asked how I was feeling, and he did not waste any time. He asked me to lie down so he could examine my breast.

I immediately said to him, "The lump is not in my breast; it is under my armpit."

He did not respond to my comment; he just began examining me around the edges of my left breast as if he were searching for something, and sure enough, he felt a lump and said to me, "This feels like *cancer*!"

I immediately responded, "*No*, it is not cancer. I have fibrocystic breasts. I do not have cancer!"

Dr. Artistry said, "I would like to do a needle biopsy to determine if this is cancer." I was shocked and instantly became numb. Dr. Artistry said, "I'll be right back." He stepped out of the examination room and came back with his assistant. He explained to me what he was about to do and how he was going to do it. He went straight to the lump without any fumbling and took two samples of breast tissue to be examined by the lab. Dr. Artistry told me it would take about three to five days before I would receive the results. He also asked if I wanted to be notified by phone, or did I want to schedule an appointment to get the results from the biopsy? I told him that I would prefer to schedule an appointment, and before leaving his office I scheduled an appointment for the following Friday.

Well, during the weekend my breast became swollen and painful, and it had turned purple and blue. It looked like a bent finger was protruding and trying to get out of my breast!

Early morning on Monday, August 16, 2010, I could not wait until the doctor's office opened so that I could report to the surgeon what the biopsy had done to my breast. So when I called the office and the doctor got on the telephone, before I could get out of my mouth what was going on, he told me that he had gotten the results back from the lab and the results revealed that I had cancer!

Dr. Artistry told me to call the oncology department and schedule an appointment. He also stated that he was going out of town and would not be available to do surgery until he returned in a couple of weeks. He mentioned that someone else could follow up with me and perform the surgery if I did not want to wait until he returned to the office.

Being that I felt Dr. Artistry knew what he was doing and was highly recommended, I told him that I wanted him to perform my surgery and I would wait until he returned. I hung up the telephone, feeling disconnected and numb!

CHAPTER 2

The Three Men God Assigned to Comfort Me

I OPENED UP THE BREAK-ROOM door and began walking down the hall into the lobby headed back to my office. As I was walking toward the entrance door to my office area, on the morning of Monday, August 16, 2010, Mr. Solace, the agency director, appeared out of nowhere. Mr. Solace said, "Good morning, how are you doing?"

As he continued to walk away, I responded with, "I have just been told that I have breast cancer!" He froze and then began walking toward me.

Mr. Solace looked me straight in the eyes and listened attentively as I cried and began telling him, "I do not know what I am going to do!" I just got back from being off work, assisting my mother with her recovery from an experience with cancer.

Being trained as a licensed spiritual practitioner and knowing the healing power of God, prayer did not even enter my mind. All that knowing and training went right out of the window! It was now my turn to stand in the absolute truth about God's healing power!

Mr. Solace began walking me to my office and getting me out of the lobby. I remember saying to him, "What am I going to do?" I had forgotten God was in charge of my life and forever with me!

I went on and on, repeating all of my fears, stating how I had just come back from being off work with my mother, and exhausted all of my vacation and sick leave balances and what about my medical and dental coverage, and how was I going to pay my mortgage? I had a list of fears that I was sharing with Mr. Solace.

He stood in my office so patiently with compassion in his eyes as strength and sensitivity had their way. Mr. Solace kept eye contact with me as I was crying releasing soul pain from the gut. Mr. Solace repeated softly, "We are here for you!" Eventually, I said to Mr. Solace that I knew he was on his way to a meeting and that he should be leaving, so that he would not be too late. Mr. Solace responded as if I said nothing, and he did not budge.

He stayed with me, allowing me to cry even more with my head about his ribs. As I think back on that moment, I feel grateful and truly blessed that God allowed Mr. Solace to be the first person I saw after Dr. Artistry shared with me over the telephone that cancer was in my left breast. The compassion, patience, and strength that Mr. Solace expressed will always be cherished. He left my office after approximately thirty minutes or so, and before he left, he asked me if I was okay with him leaving. I looked up at him and chuckled, said yes, and then thanked him for taking the time to listen and comfort me. I assured him that I was okay! He left physically, and in my heart, his compassion, patience, and strength will always remain!

After Mr. Solace left my office, I immediately thought, "Oh, my sons" and "How am I going to tell my youngest son that cancer had the nerve to come into my left breast? Divine Love! I need your help! Please give me the words to say with an attitude of victory."

I had to remind myself that God was with me, and my adult sons would handle the information just fine. I had no doubts about my oldest son, and

I was concerned about my youngest son. I had to remember that I set the tone on how they would respond!

I decided to stay at work. Work was the best place for me at the time. I sat down and talked with God. I told him how much I needed him to pull me through this health situation. I also thanked him for appointing Mr. Solace to be the first person I saw to comfort me during this life-changing experience! I also let God know that I trusted him, and I knew that he would bring me through white as snow!

About thirty minutes before it was time to get off work, I called my oldest son and told him that I was coming over after work. He said, "Okay, Mom." Kenneth had no idea that I was coming to share life-changing information.

When I got to the house, Kenneth was ironing. I walked up to him and gave him a kiss. I stood right in front of my son as he was ironing, I looked him in the eyes and starting laughing, and then out came, "Son, I was told that cancer is in my left breast."

He looked at me and said, "Mom, you are joking, right?"

I smiled and said, "No, son, I am not joking."

Kenneth looked at me and said, "Mom, you know I am here for you, right?"

I gazed at him and said, "Yes, I know." Kenneth gave me a big bear hug and said, "Mom, I love you; you are going to be fine. You know that, don't you?"

I said, "Yes, and believe, I am being healed right now!"

I left my son feeling loved, supported, and victorious. I knew without a doubt that God was healing me, and all I had to do was remember that God is a healer and provider, and I am his child. I drove home in silence. I wanted to replay in my mind the sound of strength in Kenneth's voice as he assured me that I am loved and supported.

Once I got home and prepared for bed I thought, "Tina Maria, when you told Kenneth, you did not even cry; I guess you had cried all the tears that needed to be released while sharing with Mr. Solace."

As I lay in my bed, I began to praise God again for blessing me with my son Kenneth, who comforted me and was willing and ready to ride on this journey with me. I said to myself, "I told Kenneth, and now I have to contact and share with Paul."

As I was falling asleep that night with an attitude of gratitude, knowing for sure that God and I have the victory, I began to meditate on a verse from the Bible that says something like this: "If I have faith the size of a mustard seed, whatever I speak and believe shall be done unto me, in the name of Jesus." I felt confident knowing that my faith in God is much larger than a mustard seed, and I had accepted in my heart that God is with me and we have the victory, so I meditated on the verse of faith until I dozed off and slept peacefully.

The morning after sharing with Kenneth, I thought, "Ooh, now it is Paul's turn, I better give him a call." Before picking up the telephone to call Paul, I prayed and asked Divine Love to speak through me and give me the words that no one else but Divine Love could.

After prayer I picked up the telephone and I started dialing Paul's number, and on every exhale, I asked God to speak. Well, there was no answer, so I left a voice message and then e-mailed Paul, informing him that I wanted to talk with him as soon as possible.

I received a call from Paul the following day. When I picked up the telephone and heard his voice, I immediately went into silent prayer, asking God to give me the words to say when sharing with him that *cancer* had the nerve to visit my left breast. After praying, I was totally surrendered to receiving the words that no one except God could give me to tell my youngest son that I had an unwanted visitor in my left breast that is known by the name of cancer.

Paul was chirpy and said, "Hey, Moma, I got your e-mail. What's going on?" I replied, "Well, son, I was told that cancer is in my left breast!" There was a long silence, and then Paul asked if I was okay. I told him, "Yes son, God is curing me right now."

I could hear and feel the fear and tears that Paul was trying to conceal. "Moma, are you sure you are okay? Moma, are you scared? Moma, pleeeeeeeeese let them remove your breast and do whatever has to be done in order for you to live! Moma, I cannot imagine life without you! Moma, please, please! Moma are you going to let them take your breast? Moma, please say yes."

I told Paul, "Yes, son, I prayed to God, and God revealed to me to follow the doctor's recommendation completely and know that He is guiding and is in full control of all that concerns me. I am fine. God is with me, and I have no fear!"

"Okay, Moma, do you need anything?"

"Yes, son, I would like for you to pray, believing that our prayers are manifesting right now, and most of all, keep loving me."

Paul said, "Oh, Moma, I will always love you, and of course I will pray for you every day; you can count on that!"

After talking with Paul, I felt a huge sense of relief. I said to myself, "Tina Maria, now the journey has begun, and you *better* know, like you have never known before, that the presence and power of Divine Love is in control of all that unfolds!"

CHAPTER 3

First Visit with the
Doctor of Healing

—⸙—

A FEW DAYS AFTER TALKING with my youngest son, I had the most important appointment in my life. It was my first visit with Dr. Alyson (Doctor of Healing), the oncologist. I woke up early in the morning and began preparing to meet a woman who would share a medical diagnosis and treatment plan with me that would require me to trust in the healing power of the Lord. It was time for me to totally put my life in the hands of the Doctor of Healing, knowing that God was in control of all of her decisions concerning me. The moment finally came when I walked into the medical building to meet the Doctor of Healing. I felt calm and supported, as I had several friends who accompanied me. I remember thinking,

"I have God and friends with me, and I will walk courageously on this journey to recovery!"

While checking in at the medical station, I was greeted warmly and with a beautiful smile. Before I could sit down and get comfortable, my name was called, my heart started pounding, and I became anxious.

I thought, "Oh, okay, God, now I am going to hear what is happening inside of my precious body according to medical science!" The medical assistant greeted us cheerfully; it was if she knew us.

We were taken into a large room big enough to accommodate all of us comfortably. We all had a seat, and in less than five minutes, the Doctor of Healing knocked on the door and entered. She looked me straight in the eyes and reached out her hand as I reached out mine, and as we shook hands, she introduced herself and I introduced myself, along with each one of the ladies that were with me. The handshake that I received from the Doctor of Healing made me know immediately that God had placed me in the best hands ever. Before she even opened her mouth, I could feel an energy of deep concern and determination to eliminate the unwanted visitor in my left breast.

After the introduction, I gave the Doctor of Healing my full attention. I was ready to hear exactly what the medical test revealed and what my doctor thought of the test results. As she started talking, two of the ladies started whispering at the same time. They started sharing unpleasant and unwanted information about other people they knew. It was unbelievable; they were in a conversation all to themselves! I thought, "Oh, where do they think they are?"

Eventually, Lady of Love, who is a dear friend, and who was not participating in the conversation, spoke up and told the two women that their conversation was inappropriate, and this was not the time or place to be discussing what they were discussing. They both looked at her, rolled their eyes, mumbled, and then they discontinued their conversation about death. Hearing about the death of someone else at that time was definitely not for my highest good!

After ending their conversation, they both started asking the doctor question after question concerning the diagnosis. I thought, "When am I going to get a turn?" They would not be silent! What I know today that I did not understand then was that they both were fearful about the diagnosis. Them discussing death and being talkative was possibly their way of expressing their fear.

The doctor stated that she wanted to examine me and asked the ladies to leave the room. The ladies left the room slowly and hesitantly! I told the ladies, "I will be out soon. Get out!" We all gave a slight chuckle.

As the Doctor of Healing began to examine me, I could see and sense the concern on her face, and her body language was talking loud and clear. She told me that the tumor was very large, and the cancer in my left breast was aggressive and fast growing. She said, "We are going to have to pull out the big guns for you!"

I said to myself, "I have already pulled out the big gun, God, and he is on the job right now!"

I sat there listening to the doctor tell me that cancer was in my left breast and had the ability to spread throughout my body. I immediately asked God, "Talk to me, talk to me Lord; pleeeeeeeese remind me of the absolute truth."

I heard God say, "Judge not according to appearance and what you hear. I am with you, Tina Maria!" I had to consciously be in the moment and remember that I could not allow fear to have its way!

I thought, "I cannot give fear a second in my mind, and if I do, cancer will take over my body!"

I knew that with God, all things were possible, and I was not going to allow cancer to have my body. Cancer was an unwanted visitor, and it was time for it to go, right now!

After silently talking to God, I looked at my doctor and asked, "When will I begin chemotherapy?"

She replied, "You will have surgery first to have a catheter port inserted into your right breast in order to administer the chemotherapy." She explained the procedure and possible side effects of the chemotherapy.

As she was describing possible side effects, I repeated silently, "That is not the truth about Tina Maria! My body will not have any adverse effects during chemotherapy. I declare it in the name of Jesus!"

After the doctor explained everything in detail, not missing a beat, she also gave me some instructions and pamphlets, which included more information about my temporary health condition. No, I did not read the information when I got home. I thought, "Let me immediately toss all this information in the trash. After all, that is where garbage belongs." It was not my desire to know all the details, especially since Divine Love was cleansing me!

CHAPTER 4

Asking for Prayer and Letting Cancer Know Who Is the Boss

WHILE LYING IN BED ONE early morning being present with the chirping sound of birds, accepting that they had come to me to sing a song of victory. The birds left me smiling and feeling very grateful that God had used them this morning to sing a song of victory to me! After the song of "Victory", I decided to tell some praying folks that cancer had the nerve to invade my left breast. I was mentally prepared to not only share but to ask for prayer and support during my experience with cancer.

Asking for prayer and support was a big one for me, being that I seldom ask others for prayer or support. I thought that because I had been trained as a spiritual practitioner, I knew what to do and had all the tools that were necessary to comfort myself, that I could hold my own hand. Well, common sense kicked in and reminded me that regardless of how much training, experience, and tools I thought I had as a licensed spiritual practitioner, I also deserved prayer and support from family and friends while going through a life-altering experience.

I thought, "Tina Maria, you are really good at praying and supporting others, and now it is your turn to receive prayer and support." So I picked up the telephone and allowed my fingers to exercise as they dialed every minister I knew and everybody I knew who believes in the power of prayer! I desired people praying for me who not only believed in the power of prayer but expected, along with me, a cure from God!

I was not interested in giving myself or allowing anyone else to throw me a pity party; I prayed and asked God not to allow anyone in my presence who was fearful of cancer and/or thought that I was going to die! I knew that cancer had no power over me, and without a doubt I had the victory.

I could hear the voice of Rev. Dr. Elouise Oliver reminding me that God was the only power in my life. I also heard the voices of Love, Courage, and Victory repeating in my mind with authority, "You must acknowledge cancer as being equal to a cold and not something that has power over you." I held on to the voices of Rev. Dr. Elouise Oliver, Love, Courage, and Victory as I declared with conviction that God was the only power in my life!

I reminded myself that whenever I had a cold, I did not fear the cold. I attended to it with plenty of water, juice, soup, rest, and then, eventually, it went away. I chose to know that cancer was visiting my left breast temporarily and it did not have any more power over me than a cold. I vowed to address cancer with God, chemotherapy, surgery, radiation, and tender loving care, knowing that with the power of God, I had the victory!

As I was returning home from my last doctor's appointment pertaining to the surgery to have the catheter port inserted, I began praising and talking to Divine Love.

I thanked the Master Healer for all of my doctors and the entire medical team who were involved with my healing process. I also thanked him for my insurance coverage that provided everything required for a victorious restoration.

I drove up into my garage, got out of the car, and opened the door to the home of healing. I sat down on my chocolate chaise in silence for forty-five minutes or so, and then I picked up the telephone to call a few relatives and friends. I wanted to let them know that I would be starting chemotherapy in several weeks, after I had a catheter port inserted into the upper part of my right breast. I explained that the catheter port would allow the medical staff to administer the chemotherapy into my body.

Folks wanted to know all the details of what was discussed during my visit with the Doctor of Healing. Knowing it was not for my highest good to keep repeating or embracing my medical diagnosis, I refused to repeat all the details to everyone. I decided to focus on what was my business, and my business was to know that Divine Love was loving me through the process of wholeness.

A state of courage and victory set in like crazy glue that could not be removed. As I stood tall as a redwood tree and courageous as could be, cancer could not scare me. My energy was so high, and I felt that cancer was definitely in for a surprise. I was standing tall, not bent or bowed, and talked to the unwanted visitor, letting it know that it had to go!

I informed cancer that it was not invited and could not remain in my breast or any other part of my body; it had to go, right now—not tomorrow, right now in the name of Jesus! As I was telling cancer that it had to go right now, in my mind and heart it was dissolving.

As I was compliant with the medical professionals, doing everything my doctor suggested, I never accepted that I had cancer. Now I did acknowledge that I was having an experience with cancer, which is different from having cancer. When you have something, it remains with you. When you have an experience with something, it comes and it goes. The knower in me let me know that cancer was dissolving and would never come back.

I made it my business to repeat and embrace one of my favorite affirmations: "My Body Is Young, Strong, And Healthy; It Knows It, And It Shows It" I held on to this affirmation like my life depended on it!

CHAPTER 5

Courage Before Surgery and Chemotherapy

I GOT UP ON THE morning of Wednesday, September 1, 2010, and started my daily communication with the Lord. I told the Lord, "God, today is the day that I will have a catheter port inserted into the upper part of my right breast so that chemotherapy can be administered into my body."

I also told God that fear stopped by this morning and tried to have a seat. The voice of Knowing said to me, "Tina Maria, you know that you have not been given a spirit of fear. You have been given a spirit of power, peace, love, and joy. You must stand in your power and in joy. Regardless of what you are experiencing, you must know that I am always with you!"

After prayer I felt courageous and ready to have the catheter port inserted; I left the house praising the Lord for the opportunity to have a device inserted that would contribute to saving my life.

When I arrived at the hospital, I was greeted warmly by the staff. After registering, I was taken to the surgery department. The doctor and anesthesiologist both came into my room and explained the procedure that was about to take place. They both were energized, kind, and seemed knowledgeable about what they were about to do. After meeting the two most important people during this surgery, I felt grateful that my prayer had been answered because I had asked God to choose people who were kind, knowledgeable, and joyful to attend to me before, during, and after my surgery.

I was rolled into the operating room by a young man who was very cautious with how he rolled me down the halls and into the operating room. Entering the operating room, I was greeted by more staff; there were at least six people in the operating room. I was told that some were there to observe the procedure. I was asked several questions and then medicated.

When I opened my eyes, I was in the recovery room. I began praising the Lord for bringing me through the first surgery. I lay awake for about thirty minutes, feeling grateful and ready to start a journey of restoration. I then asked the nurse to please call my mother and ask her to pick me up.

Moma arrived within twenty minutes and took me to a restaurant to have a meal. It was at my request and against her advice to go out for lunch. Moma wanted to take me straight home so that I could rest, but I insisted on eating right away! I felt so good that after the meal, Moma and I went shopping.

On the morning of September 9, 2010, I got up feeling grateful that my son, Kenneth, was escorting me to receive a treatment that would be lifesaving. I thought, "Okay, Lord, the biggest day of my life has arrived. It is time for me to have chemotherapy." I asked the Lord not to let me see it as something that could harm me; instead, let me embrace it as healing water.

After getting dressed and talking to God, I went into the kitchen and prepared some goodies to take with me to eat just in case I got hungry while the healing water was being administered for several hours into my body.

As soon as I finished preparing my goodies, I heard my front door open. I looked up at the golden clock, and I heard Kenneth say, "Hi, Moma, I'm here."

As we drove into the parking lot of the hospital, I said to myself, "Okay, healing water, here I come!" Knowing that my attitude would affect my experience, I decided to focus on how blessed I was to receive the healing water and to have my son by my side. As Kenneth got out of the truck and came around to the passenger side of his vehicle, he opened the door, reached for my hand, and escorted me to the infusion clinic. Kenneth asked how I felt. I chuckled and said, "Son, I feel blessed, and I am ready to go get some healing water!"

As we walked into the building and headed for the infusion clinic, I felt peaceful and secure knowing that Kenneth would be with me as I received chemotherapy. I arrived at my destination and stood in line. When it was my turn to register, I walked up to the counter and was greeted by a woman with a smile that could light up the world. She was joy filled and friendly, as if she knew me and was glad to see me again.

As soon as I sat down, I thought that greeting was as if she knew me! Immediately, I said thank you Lord! I knew that my prayer was in action. I had prayed that my experience with the medical staff during my journey of recovery would be one of warmth and joy. And that is just what I received from the young woman who registered me. Yay!

I heard my name, Tina Maria, I stood up, and the nurse and I greeted each other with a smile. She took me into a room that was enclosed, different from the other spaces where chemotherapy was being administered. I walked into a space that felt like a room: it had walls, a swivel television, and room to move around in, unlike the other spaces in the infusion clinic. I thought, "Oh, this is nice, clean, and I have some privacy. Yay!"

The nurse told me to get comfortable, and before she put the IV into the catheter port to begin treatment, she explained in detail the different medications that were going to be administered by IV and why. She did not miss a step, which I appreciated.

The royal treatment had begun. The medical staff showed compassion, empathy, and was kind as could be. They repeatedly asked if I was warm enough, if I needed something to snack on, how was I feeling, and they were even available for brief conversations.

It was several medical personnel who checked on me throughout the treatment. They all were ready and willing to comfort me as I wished. I remember crying tears of joy due to the wonderful encounters that I had with the medical staff.

The atmosphere made me think about when I would visit with a friend or family member, how they would cater to me during my visit with them. I felt so grateful and blessed to have such a warm and joyous experience. As I lay in the infusion clinic for many hours receiving my healing water, being catered to as a queen, I was constantly praising the Lord for inspiring his children to treat me as family.

What really touched my heart was that each time I arrived for treatment, from the first day until the last day, I was always greeted warmly and felt as though the staff was happy to see me. I will always remember and be grateful to the medical staff for treating me as family and, most of all, I give thanks to God for answering my prayer.

CHAPTER 6

Cancer Provoked My Stepfather's Death the Day after My First Chemotherapy Treatment

It was September 10, 2010, the day after my first chemotherapy treatment. I received a call stating that my stepfather had died. I instantly became numb. Before the telephone call, I had been feeling off-balance, nauseated, and dizzy; I also had chills, due to chemotherapy the day before.

I talked with Moma over the telephone, but I did not go over to my parents' home. It was just a bit too much for me to handle. Hearing that Terry was gone was one thing, but to go over to his home and not have him be physically there would have brought me to my knees! The natural thing for me to do was to go and be with my mother, but I told myself, "Tina Maria, you must take care of yourself; you just had chemotherapy yesterday; you need to relax. Do not go over to the house!"

After hanging up the telephone, I remember asking the Lord, "Lord, for real? Did you really have to take Terry home a day after I had my healing water administered?" I allowed my tears to flow as long as they wanted to, and then I went down memory lane to Terry's and my conversation when I told him that I went to the doctor and was told that cancer was visiting my left breast.

Terry had asked me, "What did the doctor say; does it look good? Are you going to make it?"

Before he could say anything else, I had said, "Yes, I am going to make it, and you are, too! Let's know together that we are both being healed right now in the name of Jesus!"

Terry looked me in the eyes, smiled, and said, "Let me give you a hug" and held me tight. We both became silent and allowed the silence to speak out loud as Terry embraced me as his child.

My mother was told several years ago that her husband would not be here with us very long due to his medical condition. Well, because we were praying and he lived many years past what my mother had been told, I guess I thought he would just keep on living! I was wrong.

My stepdad also had an experience with the unwanted visitor, which eventually destroyed his physical body. Unfortunately, cancer had the nerve to take my stepdad's life like a thief in the night, the day after my first chemotherapy treatment.

It was so important for me to stay focused and positive, knowing that my attitude contributed to the success of my treatments. I knew that prayer was the best and only support that I could give to myself and my family.

I remember praying and asking Divine Love to give my family strength and peace as they handled Terry's service without me. I decided it would be for my highest good not to get involved with the planning of Terry's "home going" service. I was so grateful God sent Kenneth and others to assist Moma with facilitating a beautiful "home going" celebration for my stepdad.

It was definitely a relief for me that someone else was handling the service arrangements. It allowed me to be present with myself and what I was physically feeling after having my first chemotherapy treatment.

I stayed prayed up and said my daily affirmations. I refused to let fear come into my thoughts and stay, not even for a minute. I had to tell myself that just because Divine Love took my dad home did not mean he was going to take me home right now! I said repeatedly, "I am going to live and be joy filled!" As I affirmed and embraced these words each time, I got louder and louder, knowing that my body believed every word that I said and felt and would respond accordingly. After affirming and embracing, "I am going to live and be joy filled," I was able to smile and felt without a doubt that I was not going to die due to cancer being in my left breast!

Unfortunately, I could not attend Terry's service. I had to remind myself that he was at peace now, and I had to take care of myself. So I stayed home and had my own private service, remembering and cherishing the times Terry and I shared.

I began to think about the time we had together over the last year of his life. One of the most sacred memories was when I took Terry to have a medical procedure done on his liver, and I stayed with him the whole time. I helped him tie his gown and get comfortable in the bed, and I held his hands as I prayed. Eventually it was time for him to have surgery, so I went into the waiting room lobby, sat down, closed my eyes, and began to pray and meditate. After praying and meditating for some time, I felt peaceful and knew that the outcome of the surgery would be for my dad's highest good.

Another precious memory is when I had just became a first-time home buyer and wanted to replace the linoleum in the guest bathroom. I drove us to Home Depot and purchased all the materials and supplies needed to replace the linoleum. When we returned to my home, Terry joyfully instructed and assisted me with how to rip out the old and put down the new. I did most of the ripping. During this home repair project, Terry was weak and did not have the strength to do heavy labor, so I did most of the work.

As Terry was smiling and giving instructions, I was complaining about how tired and sore I was from pulling, bending, and so on. I remember saying, "Now I understand why contractors charge what they do because this is hard work." We both laughed.

Under any other circumstance, I would not have been doing this type of labor, but since Terry was assisting me, I felt that I could do it. I felt grateful and very proud of myself for being willing to do something that could be done with Terry's assistance instead of paying a contractor to do it for me.

After going down memory lane, I said a thanksgiving prayer. I thanked the Lord for Terry sharing his knowledge, time, compassion, patience, joy, and love. I will cherish the moments we had together and most of all, I will always remember the joy I felt when Terry told me how proud and honored he was to have me as his daughter.

CHAPTER 7

My Hair Released Itself from My Head

∽

My hair released itself from my head eighteen days after my first chemotherapy treatment. It was the morning of September 27, 2010, seven days after my oldest son's birthday.

I had gotten up later than usual, and I was expecting my daughter-in-law to come over to spend several hours with me. It was about 10:00 a.m. when the doorbell rang. I got out of bed slowly, as I was feeling nauseated and weak. I made it to my front door and opened it to greet Jasmine, lovingly known to me as Daughter of Joy.

Jasmine had brought us some Jamba Juice. I saw the juice and instantly felt energized. I embraced Jasmine with a kiss on the cheek. She walked into my roomy, sunlit kitchen and put the drinks down on the island. As Jasmine was putting the Jamba Juice down, I told her that I was going to shower and would be out soon.

When I entered the shower, the water felt soothing and warm, with the perfect amount of pressure landing on my head. As I put my fingers through my hair as I was washing it, my hair embraced my fingers and released itself into the palms of my hands and laced my fingers.

As I looked at my hands and saw my hair, I started screaming and crying at the top of my lungs. "Jasmine! Jasmine! My hair!"

Jasmine busted through the bathroom door and said, "What, Mom? Are you okay? What is the matter?" Her eyes were as big as a baby deer's!

I was crying and screaming, "My hair! My hair is falling out, and it's all gone!"

As I was crying and screaming, "My hair, my hair is gone," Jasmine (bless her heart) grabbed me and held me tight as the water soaked both of us.

Jasmine held me and said, "Ooh, Mom, I am so sorry!" We both cried as she embraced me tightly.

After some time, I calmed down, and then Jasmine said, "Come on, Mom, get out of the shower, and I will clean the tub for you!"

I replied, "I can clean it."

She said lovingly, "No, Mom, I am going to clean it for you!" I surrendered and allowed her to clean the tub, removing the hair that did not go down the drain as it released itself from my head.

Thinking back, I thought I had prepared myself mentally for when my hair would release itself from my head due to the chemotherapy. When I was told that my hair would fall out, I had cut my hair as short as I could. I felt that if my hair was going to come out, I would take it off and not the chemotherapy.

I meditatively sectioned out my hair, and as I began to cut my shoulder-length hair off my head, I apologized and told my hair what I was doing and why. I also thanked my hair for contributing to my warmth and beauty. Several days after cutting my hair, I called my daughter-in-law Dominique (Daughter of Determination) and asked her to come over and cut off all of the hair that I could not grasp.

Being that I had a talk with my hair and I had reminded myself of how my hair grew back, when I had colored it blond and cut it to less than an inch, believing that blondes have more fun! I had told myself that it would grow back, like it did before, and I would still be beautiful with no hair on my head.

Well, needless to say that when my hair released itself from my head on September 27, 2010, I did not remember a word I had told myself in preparation for my hair loss. I had temporarily forgotten the reassurance I had given myself before a part of me was gone.

As I think back on that morning, I give thanks and remember what my Nana used to say: "Baby, God never leaves us alone." My blessing was I was not alone; just as Nana had said, God had sent Jasmine to be with me when all of my hair released itself and went down the drain.

I am so grateful that God comforted me through Jasmine at one of the most life-changing moments a woman could ever have.

God knew exactly what he was doing by having me stay in bed longer than I should have, knowing that Jasmine was coming to visit. Now I know the reason why I laid in bed longer; it was because God wanted Jasmine to experience my hair loss with me. I remember thanking the Lord for sending Jasmine, who knew how to comfort me. Not only did she hold me; she prayed for me and lovingly cleaned out the tub for me!

As soon as Jasmine (Daughter of Joy), left, I put on Yolanda Adams's CD and turned the volume up as loud as I could stand it and played the song titled "I Gotta Believe" over and over as I cried and sung along. After there were no more tears, I began praising Divine Love for gifting the world with Yolanda Adams and anointing her with healing power through the use of her voice.

CHAPTER 8

Surrendered to Having My Left Breast Removed

THE EVENING BEFORE HAVING MY left breast removed, I took a long meditative soak from neck
to toe, explaining to my breasts what was going
to happen in the morning. As I explained why the
left breast had to be removed, I welcomed tears;
actually, I tried to cry, but no tears would appear.

Now I had given myself permission to cry,
scream, and just totally fall apart, being that,
early the next morning, my beautiful breast that
rested near my heart would be gone. Instead,
peace and strength embraced me so tight that I
could not cry or feel sad; all I could do was be still
and feel the peace of the Lord.

Shortly after I stepped out of the tub, the
phone started ringing off the hook with blessings

of love and radiant health being bestowed upon me. The last call that came through before I turned off the telephone ringer was from Rev. Joan Steadman, who set the tone for me to remember who and what I am in God.

After speaking with Rev. Joan Steadman, there was one call I had to make—one that provoked total surrender. It was an affirmative Chamber of Prayer conference call, one that sealed me with an enormous amount of peace, relaxation, and joy!

I called into the conference line that was set up just for me. As I sat on the telephone and heard each click informing me that a Prayer Angel was joining in, love and peace embraced me. I felt lighter and lighter during every click. I could feel the love and support from all five Prayer Angels. Once everyone was on the call, the Chamber of Prayer began!

A Chamber of Prayer is when everyone is praying affirmatively together out loud, without begging or pleading, just knowing that there is a loving presence in the universe—God—and we are one with God, declaring and affirming, giving thanks, and expecting what has been affirmed. Then we release the declaration into the power of God. It was an experience that I still do not have words for! All I know is there was a knowing and peace that comforted me. Every cell in my body believed every word that was spoken and responded accordingly.

Knowing and accepting that love is a healer, there was not any other option for my body other than to reveal radiant health and wholeness. Every cell in my body knew what to do and how to do it in order for harmony and wholeness to be restored, and it did! I felt strong and loved, and I knew that my physical life would not be over anytime soon—no way, no how!

I slept so peacefully, like a newborn baby child, and woke up the next morning on January 18, 2011, full of energy and acceptance of my left breast being removed forever.

After surgery, I remember thinking, "Ooh, I must have been on cloud joy!" I woke up from surgery feeling grateful that I could feel all of my senses. I remember thinking that the pain and nausea I was feeling were present to let me know I am alive! I also woke up to the gift of a friend greeting me as I opened my eyes.

Once again, God was reminding me through my friend Lady B that I was not alone. As I opened my eyes, I could see her adjusting the covers and covering me up. I remember thinking, "I must have been dancing in my sleep and moved all the covers off me!" It was comforting to awaken with a friend caring for me.

When Lady B started walking out of the hospital room, "Grateful," a song on Karen Drucker's CD *Songs of the Spirit III*, started playing in my mind. I embraced the words with every cell of my body. I began humming some of the lyrics. After humming for a short time, it was definitely on; it was thanksgiving and praise time; it was time to give thanks for waking me up from surgery and having Lady B there to comfort me!

CHAPTER 9

Radiation and Fear

$\sim$

ONCE AGAIN I WAS GREETED warmly by some of the most caring medical professionals I had ever met. I got undressed from head to waist and put on a gown that was given to me by a cheerful young woman.

Surprisingly, as I sat in the waiting area, waiting for my name to be called, fear stopped by and said, "Tina Maria, I'm here!" And then suddenly a young man opened the door and greeted me, asking me to please come with him. I could not move; it was like I was stuck to the chair. I mean stuck—I sat there for seemingly five minutes or so; I could not move!

The young man looked at me and smiled as he asked, "Are you coming?"

All I could do was look at him, and then eventually I said yes. He stood there with the door wide open patiently for approximately another two or three minutes. I slowly got up and followed him into the area where I was going to receive radiation.

The young man took his time and explained to me how and what was going to happen. As he was explaining to me what was going to happen, I was greeted by another cheerful medical technician. She introduced herself as she reached out her hand to embrace mine. She began explaining the machine that provided the radiation and the dos and don'ts during the treatment. She took me through the process, step by step, as she also showed concern about my physical and mental state.

I was told when to be still, inhale, and hold my breath, and when to let my breath go. After each time I inhaled and exhaled my breath, I was asked if I was okay with sincerity. The kindness and compassion I received during my radiation treatment helped to dissolve the fear that had me unmovable.

When I got home from having my first radiation treatment, I had to have a talk with myself. I said, "Tina Maria, what happened? Why were you afraid and could not move? What thoughts were you having to cause you to allow fear to visit you?"

I had to acknowledge that I felt violated, which caused me to have resistance to accepting the radiation treatment. I also had to honor what I was feeling, and then I had to make a choice about how I would view having radiation, because I had many more treatments to accept before the recommended treatment plan was completed.

I knew that if I did not release the fear, it would make my treatments unpleasant, and I definitely did not want that to happen. So, I went within and allowed all beliefs that did not serve my highest good to come up and out so that I could continue the treatments without hesitation or fear. I decided to accept radiation as my friend and not a violator.

After going within and acknowledging my feelings, praying, and accepting radiation as a friend that would help me to stay on this physical plane called Earth, I was looking forward to my next treatment. I wanted to run into the room where radiation was given.

Of course, running was all in my mind. Due to the pain and weakness I was experiencing in my legs, I was not able to run physically. But at least I was running in my mind and knew that one day I would be able to run again if I wanted to.

After praying a prayer of thanksgiving for radiation, being one of the healing methods that would assist me with remaining here in the visible, I was totally unafraid and looked forward to the remaining treatments with a heart filled with gratitude for Dr. Ally, who is the radiation doctor God used to prescribe the radiation treatments.

The blessing during radiation was I never experienced severe burning or peeling of my skin. I also got a dot tattoo that was placed in the center of my chest as part of the treatment. The radiation machine was lined up with the tattoo in order to make sure I received radiation in the appropriate area. I acknowledged the tattoo as a blessing. The dot symbolizes a period, which means it is done, it is finished, and it is complete!

CHAPTER 10

Reasonable-Accommodation Job Reassignment and Forgiveness

I HAD BEEN BACK AT work for at least two years, recovering slowly and surely, when I was informed that I was going to be reassigned in order to continue accommodating my reasonable-accommodations request. I had never considered that one of the most important things in my life, which was serving as a community health outreach worker, would be taken away from me due to an experience with breast cancer.

The treatments that were used to get rid of the uninvited visitor known as cancer also often left me in extreme discomfort and with physical limitations.

I could not install car seats for our children, due to the pain that I experienced in my left arm, legs, and both feet, caused by lymphedema in my arm and polyneuropathy in my feet. I had limitations with standing, pushing, pulling, and being out in extreme weather, which prevented me from being able to recertify, and keep my certification, as a certified child passenger safety technician, which was a requirement for my position as a community health outreach worker.

Being that providing car-seat education and demonstrating the proper way to install a car seat was not a daily assignment, I did not think that it would cause me to be transferred to another department under reasonable accommodations, especially since approximately 98 percent of my time was facilitating senior and childhood injury-prevention presentations.

I was not happy about leaving our elders and children. I suggested that I stay with the department and continue to provide senior and childhood injury prevention presentations, and not be a certified child passenger safety technician, being that there were four other employees that were also technicians. I was told no, that I could no longer be accommodated in the position that I was in, which broke my heart. I had been with my employer for almost twenty-five years and served as a community health outreach worker for the last eleven-plus years.

I truly enjoyed going into senior housing facilities, libraries, churches, and senior centers, presenting information to our elders on fall prevention, driving safely, and personal emergency preparedness. I also loved going into the elementary schools and speaking with our children about the bicycle helmet law and safety rules that must be followed when they are riding on their wheeled vehicles. All of my presentations were fun and interactive by use of "show and tell."

Of course I felt sad and angry about having to leave a position that I had so much passion for. I had truly forgotten that God is in the midst of all things, and everything will work out for my highest good and to look for the blessing in the reasonable-accommodation job reassignment with less pay.

One Sunday, I was in conversation with Rev. Sheila Gautreaux who teaches forgiveness. I shared with her that I was going to have a job reassignment with less pay. She listened attentively and with empathy and then reminded me that I must release the anger and sadness ASAP because it was not good for my health. She asked if I was willing to forgive, and I responded with a resounding yes!

The Minister of Forgiveness offered me the gift of support during the forgiveness process if needed; she then recommended a forgiveness worksheet with instructions, which she sent to me in a timely manner. I reviewed the worksheet and instructions and then ordered the forgiveness book right away.

I was serious about releasing the thoughts and emotions that were not benefiting my health, so when the book arrived, I started my forgiveness process immediately.

After reading the forgiveness book and completing all the assignments on the forgiveness worksheet, I said to myself, "I have read several books on forgiveness, and none have penetrated and transformed me like this one: *Radical Forgiveness*, by Colin Tipping."

The forgiveness book and worksheet were great reminders that we are here in the physical world as spiritual beings with assignments to help one another grow, and that no one is here to take anything away from me, which was something I had temporarily forgotten when I was told about the reasonable-accommodation job reassignment with less pay.

One of the many blessings in my reassignment was before I reported to my new job as a specialist clerk 1, my new supervisor, Aimee N. Labat, sent me a cheerful e-mail, welcoming me and stating that she and my coworkers were looking forward to my arrival and me being a part of the team.

The welcome e-mail provoked tears of appreciation for my new supervisor and my coworkers. One thing I know for sure is that God is in the midst of all situations, working it out for the good of all, and nothing can ever happen without God's approval. I'm so grateful that God is truly the decision maker!

CHAPTER 11

God's Abundant Blessings Fell Upon Me

࿐

GOD, THANK YOU FOR THE many blessings you show-
ered upon me through so many people and situations. I'm going to recall several blessings that were
life changing for me.

Blessing #1

I remember one Sunday afternoon I was looking forward to having lunch with a longtime friend, and at
the last minute, she called and informed me that she
could not have lunch with me due to unforeseen cir-
cumstances. Lady C stated that her son was going to
pick me up and take me to lunch. I was a little disap-
pointed that I was not going to spend time with Lady

C, and I also felt very grateful that her son, Paul, was going to spend the afternoon with me over lunch.

I knew I was in for a treat, being that Paul loves the Lord, and I do, too. I knew I would enjoy spending time talking about the goodness of the Lord with Paul. I'm happy to say I received more than a treat. When Paul arrived, I was looking out of the window, and as he was walking up to the door, I opened it. Paul said, "Hi, Ms. Tina, how are you feeling?" Then before we left for lunch, Paul said, "Ms. Tina, I want to pray with you." He delivered such a beautiful prayer, it made my heart smile. I felt so proud of this young man, who prayed with confidence and conviction! After receiving such a powerful prayer, I was definitely ready for lunch! I put on my coat and hat, and then Paul escorted me out of the door.

Paul's arm and mine interlocked as he escorted me to the car. He opened the car door and waited patiently as I got into the car. I thought, "This young man not only knows how to pray, he is a gentleman, ooh." My heart was really smiling!

We arrived at the restaurant, and Lady C's son got out of the car and opened the car door and again waited patiently as I got out of the car. We interlocked arms as he escorted me into the restaurant. It felt like all eyes were on us! I imagined folks could have been thinking, "Look at the mature woman on the arms of that young, strong, and handsome man." Yes, I held my head up high, and I was trying to strut, the best I could, considering I was experiencing some physical discomfort as I was walking.

Paul and I were seated, and he ordered our meal. As we were waiting for our food to arrive, I had a great time discussing the goodness of the Lord with Paul. When the meal arrived, he blessed the food and we began to eat. The food tasted so good! I believe the food tasted so good because of the wonderful company I was in!

After having a wonderful meal, I was taken home, and once again, before Paul left, he held my hands and prayed for me, leaving me with words of encouragement.

As I watched Paul drive off, I could not wait to call his mother so that I could compliment her on what an outstanding job she had done showing her son how to treat a woman and also to thank her for asking him to spend time with me.

Well, Lady C had news for me when she said, "I did not ask Paul to spend time with you and take you to lunch. Paul told me that he was going to pick you up and take you to lunch!"

I was speechless; my eyes welled up with tears of gratitude. I was so grateful that Paul thought enough of me to want to spend his Sunday afternoon to share time, a meal, and to pray for me. I said to myself, "He could have been doing so many thing on a Sunday, and he decided to spend his afternoon with me; what a blessing!" I was on a natural high for months after spending time with Paul. Even now, several years later, when I think about the Sunday that God blessed me with the gift of being in the presence of Paul Walker, I still feel a natural high!

Blessing # 2

It was on a cold, wet, stormy day in December that God showed up and showed out, inspiring Valerie Ramirez, her family, and a friend to visit me with cheers and food that provided nourishment for my body. It was not just a visit. They came to bring the spirit of joy at Christmastime to my home! As they stood outside my front door singing Christmas carols, the little girl in me became energized! I felt joy shut up in my bones! To witness the adults singing

Christmas carols was a blessing that brought joy, and to witness two little girls under the age of ten singing Christmas carols to me was truly the gift of gifts. Lord, I thank you for knowing what to do, and who to do it through! This Christmas blessing will always make my heart smile.

Blessing #3

Dear God, I thank you for a home that keeps me feeling grateful during my recovery from the uninvited visitor known as breast cancer. My home provides me with warmth, peace, and beauty, which are instrumental to my relaxation after receiving my healing treatments. I love lying on the large, cushy, golden couch and looking at the fire, as my heart embraces the warmth and beauty. The yellow, red, blue, white, and orange flames seem to call my name, gently saying, "Relax, Tina Maria, relax."

Father, God, I can feel your presence, showing up as fire, keeping me warm, relaxed, and reminding me that you are in the midst of all things, seen and unseen. I'm grateful that the home of healing is just minutes away from the medical facilities that I attend for doctor's appointments, lab work, chemotherapy, and radiation. The blessing is, after the treatments, I can go home to a warm, peaceful, and beautiful environment—a home with high ceilings, and every time I look up at the ceilings, they remind me that you, God, are raising me up and out of the health situation that I am temporarily experiencing.

God, I thank you for the many mornings I awaken and am greeted with a love song by birds. They come to my bedroom window and assertively hit against the window and sing. I lie in my bed, with tears of gratitude running down my face, knowing it's you, Lord, using the birds to comfort me and bring a smile to my face. I love waking up in the mornings, hearing the birds singing so beautifully just for me!

After three grateful years of being a first-time homeowner and living near my mother, I believe it's time to sell the home of healing, due to the lengthy commute to and from work. I am totally willing to release my home lovingly with memories of peace, beauty, birds, and trees that you allowed to comfort me.

Lord, I know that I said I should sell my home due to the commute, but deep down in my heart, I feel that my stay here was specifically for the healing of my temporary experience with breast cancer.

Now that I have completed all of my treatments and feel so much better, I accept that it is time to allow someone else to be blessed by living in the home that is entangled with peace, love, and beauty!

When many said that it could not be done, Lord, you did it! You blessed me and sold the home of healing the traditional way, within sixty days.

I remember making a firm decision, in 2012, to sell my home. I had at least five realtors advise me to list my home as a short sale due to the real-estate climate.

I thought a short sale was only for people who were having difficulty paying their mortgage. I had never been late or missed a mortgage payment, so in my mind, I had no reason to sell my home as a short sale.

Well, I must admit, after receiving the same information from folks who were in the business of selling homes, for about thirty minutes or so I thought maybe I should list my home as a short sale. All I knew was I had to do something soon because the two-hour fifteen-minute commute was too overwhelming.

I had temporarily forgotten that God was in charge of selling my home. I had forgotten that the conditions of the real-estate climate were God's business, and my business was to know, without a doubt, that God would sell my home the traditional way!

I shared with my friend Godfrey Wilson that I was going to sell my home, and I was willing to list it as a short sale. Well, the look on Wilson's face said to me, "You must have lost your mind!" He looked at me, turning his head from side to side, and said, "You don't have to sell your home as a short sale."

My response to Wilson was, "You are absolutely right! I don't have to sell my home as a short sale!"

The look on Wilson's face encouraged me to be determined to find someone who believed in the selling power of God and was willing to list my home the traditional way.

Well, God directed me to Charlotte Saulter, who is a Christian real-estate broker. I contacted Charlotte, and during our conversation, I said to her that I was interested in working with someone who believed in the power of God and would know with me that my home would sell without being sold as a short sale. Charlotte said to me with confidence, "I will sell your home!" She told me what she needed from me, what she was going to do for me, and how she was going to get it done. Charlotte did not miss a beat. She was kind, professional, and met all the deadlines, as she was present during each phase of selling the home of healing.

I have been blessed that God used Godfrey Wilson to shake me up, and I am also grateful that, along with him, Barbara Lynn, and many others who believe in the power of prayer stood with me and knew that my home was already sold in the mind of God.

God, I thank you for Charlotte Saulter, the Christian real-estate broker who rescued me from the commute. She did exactly what she said she would do. I am happy to say that I had only one open house. It was on Sunday, September 16, 2012, and escrow closed on November 16, 2012! Yes, God did it when others said it could not be done!

Blessing # 4

Lord, you blessed me with excellent health care. I feel so very blessed to have had the best medical team that anyone would have wanted to encourage me while on my journey with breast cancer. Lord, and then you put the icing on the cake by having

Jennifer Milne, CMF, CFM at Marzel's Inc., show me kindness, as she took the time to fit me with my garments and a prosthesis as if she were fitting herself. She wanted everything to be perfect with my fitting, just like me. I am grateful that Dr. Alyson, Jennifer Milne, and my health care insurance were all in agreement that a custom-fit left breast prosthesis was for my highest good.

Lord, I say "Hallelujah!" until I just can't say it any more for Dr. Alyson, who is respectfully known to me as the Doctor of Healing, whom you prescribed my medications and healing treatments through. I am also grateful for the compassion that was received from the oncology pharmacist Masha SH Lam, as she and Dr. Alyson were a team. They both were so kind, extremely patient, and returned all of my telephone calls promptly. Lord, you used their minds and hearts to assist with relieving some of the physical discomfort and saving my life, and now I stand victoriously and declare that the love you have for me has healed me totally!

Blessing #5
Lord, lots of alone time with you for approximately nine months was truly a gift. Yes, there were times

when I wished someone was there to hold and assist me. I now know that the nine months with lots of alone time was necessary in order for me to surrender and depend on you totally as you strengthened my faith, body, and character.

I am grateful for the many opportunities to praise you, Father, in the midst of discomfort and for the many comforting and healing methods I used to remain peaceful in the midst of discomfort.

I used traditional prayer, the kind of prayer that my mother and grandmother taught me. Yes, there were times when I got on my knees and reminded God of what he promised me, and then there were times when I prayed affirmatively, the way that Rev. Dr. Elouise Oliver taught me. There were times when I listened to music, meditated, contemplated on the Word of God, played my drums, and sung too!

Lord, I am grateful that you provoked your children to send me get-well cards. My front door, bedroom doors, and hallway counter were covered with 151 cards. The cards energized me and reminded me that I am loved. There were times when it was difficult to walk due to the pain in my legs and feet, and I would pray myself all the way to the mailbox, with a smile in my heart, and played a guessing game of whom I would receive a card from today because I knew there would be a card from either Valerie Street, Essie Johnson, Francell Haskins and my coworkers, Gloria Alexander, or Noel Houser, and someone else for me!

One day I received a card from Colleen Campbell that said something like, "Cancer Better Watch Out, Because It Does Not Know Who It Is Messing With."

I placed my hand on my right hip, laughed out loud, and declared, "That's right; cancer sure don't know who it is messing with!" The cards that I received from everybody definitely helped to speed up my recovery.

Lord, I am grateful that you inspired folks to call, bring food, and send gifts. I also cherished the constant communication with Rev. Dr. Margaret Stortz and Dorothy Mendez, who always made themselves available to give words of encouragement and pray affirmatively with me. Lord, you also touched the heart and mind of Lady Dianne who kept all of my coworkers informed of my progress and would call me on most Sundays and allowed me to listen to her pastor deliver a healing prayer during their prayer time. There were times when I was not able to answer the phone, and she would leave the healing prayer on voice mail, which was truly a blessing.

Lord, then you decided to show up and show out again by having Susan Brecker call me many times just to say, "I love you." Lord, I just cannot thank you enough for also inspiring Susan to suggest, while having chemotherapy, to accept it as "Healing Water" entering my body.

During chemotherapy I visualized, meditated, and accepted chemotherapy as healing water gently flowing in and then out of my body. As I lay there totally convinced that the healing water was for my highest good, sometimes I was able to fall asleep, and when I did, I slept peacefully while receiving chemotherapy.

My heart also basks in gratitude toward the people who prayed for me and expected a full recovery: Mr. Alex Briscoe, Sr. Pastor Felix Golden and First Lady Indrani Golden, Rev. Mary Armstead, Mother Juanita Bond, Catherine Landry, Olga Martinez, Delores Richard, Bonnie Lovette, NP, Sharon Porter, Jasmine King Bush, Rev. Sunshine Michelle Coleman, Paris Michael Page, Richard Scott, Zandra Washington, Richard Noel Allen Jr, Lourean Sanders, Reba Adams, Constance Ward, Lita C. DeSeville, La Rhonda Crosby Johnson, Robyn Rice Olmstead, Brother-to-Brother faith-based community group,

Jacqueline Bess, Carretha Walker and family, Yvonne Renee, Cleo Dixon, Karin Peterson, Jacquie Onipede and Jautan Stancill and family. All of these people, as well as everyone who showed up to shower love upon me at Rev. Rebecca Williams's home for the Chamber of Prayer luncheon. Lord, I can't thank you enough for all the folks within my spiritual communities and many others.

Blessing # 6

Lord, I give thanks for the love and support of my children, Kenneth Eugene King Jr. and Paul Orlando Scott Jr., and my mother, Beverly Jean Jefferson-Daste. Lord, I say "Hallelujah" until I just can't say it anymore for gifting me with family.

My heart smiles when I think back and remember the nights Moma spent with me after each chemotherapy appointment to comfort and care for me.

Kenneth has been there courageously, allowing his strength and love to embrace us all. Kenneth's wife, Mrs. Dominique King, has been there like a tree, giving love and support constantly.

I also give thanks for Paul, who prayed continuously and so passionately. Lord, my prayer to you is that my children and mother feel the love and appreciation that I have for them way down deep in their bones!

Lord, as you already know, while I was growing inside of my mother's womb, she was diagnosed with toxemia, and at some point in her pregnancy, my parents were told that I was dead. The doctors wanted to perform surgery. I am so grateful that you encouraged my mother to follow her motherly intuition and tell the doctor and my father that she knew her baby was alive and she was not going to have surgery! Lord, you stepped in once again and saved me! Now I can walk this land, following your plan, holding the hands of many, and allowing your love, joy, and kindness to shine through me and as me. Father, I vow to live out the rest of my life victoriously, knowing you are with me always and forever. "Glory Hallelujah!"

About the Author

Tina Maria was born into Christianity and completed five years of education and training to become a Licensed Spiritual Practitioner. She lives her life embracing the teachings of Jesus as well as spiritual-life principles. Tina Maria has prayed for and held the hands of many who embrace that there is a power for good in the universe, and we are all one with this power, which is God, and that we can use the power of God for our highest good.

Tina Maria proclaims that embracing the teachings of Jesus and also using spiritual-life principles is what has kept her focused on the love and healing power of God while experiencing a life-altering journey with breast cancer. Tina Maria gratefully embraces being the author God used to share *One Breast to Love and Living Life Victoriously.*

Tina Maria is available for speaking engagements and workshops. She can be contacted at: Abundant 1 Tina Maria Scott, P.O.Box 474, San Leandro, California 94577, abundanttm@gmail.com and www.facebook.com/abundant1tinamariascott.